FOREST FC PEOPLE

GEORGE BURNEY (1818–1885)
AND HIS FIGHT TO SAVE EPPING FOREST

BY

RICHARD MORRIS, OBE

Verderer of Epping Forest

LOUGHTON AND DISTRICT
HISTORICAL SOCIETY
2012

© Loughton and District Historical Society
2012

ISBN 978–1–905269–16–7

First published in 2012 by Loughton and District Historical Society
and available from
Forest Villa, Staples Road, Loughton, Essex IG10 1HP

www.loughtonhistoricalsociety.org.uk

No part of this publication may be reproduced, stored in a retrieval system, or transmitted in any form or by any means, electronic, mechanical, photocopying, recording or otherwise, without the prior written permission of the author and the copyright owner.

Cover design and plates by Artform, Little Tew, Oxon
Text design, typesetting and production and by Ted Martin

Typeset in 11/13pt Linotype Palatino

Printed in Great Britain by
Blackwell Print Ltd
Great Yarmouth

Contents

Illustrations ~ 4
Acknowledgements ~ 5

Introduction ~ 6
Early life ~ 6
Marriage ~ 7
Children ~ 8
Burney & Company Ltd ~ 9

The Fight to Save Epping Forest ~ 10
Protests against enclosures ~ 10
The Metropolitan Board of Works ~ 11
The Commons Preservation Society – East of London Local Committee ~ 12
The Epping Forest Preservation Society ~ 14
Parliament and the Courts become involved~ 15
Direct action ~ 16
Court cases ~ 19
A Commoner in Loughton ~ 22
Burney pamphlets ~ 22

Recognition ~ 25
Death ~ 27

(Plates: between pages 30 and 31)

Appendices ~ 31
*Appendix 1: Parody upon Scott's 'Lochinvar',
by John Bedford, addressed to George Burney ~ 31*
Appendix 2: Sources ~ 32
Appendix 3: Census Records ~ 34

Illustrations

Front cover: Silver *épergne* presented to George Burney in 1880
Inside front cover: Map of the Mellish estate, Isle of Dogs (1893) showing Burney's Iron tank works
Rear cover: Detail from the *épergne* presented to George Burney in 1880

PLATES
(between pages 30 and 31)

Plate 1. St George-in-the-East Church, Stepney, where George Burney, his brother and five sisters were baptised.

Plate 2. Advertisement for Burney & Co products.

Plate 3. All Saints Church, Poplar where George Burney was a member of the Vestry in the 1850s and 1860s.

Plate 4. The Crown Inn, Loughton, c1890, where Burney and his 'gang' had lunch in January 1878, after pulling fences down. (Lopping Hall is shown in the background.)

Plate 5. Terracotta panel of the 'Loughton Lopper', above the entrance to Lopping Hall. George Burney was one of the first Trustees of the Lopping Endowment.

Plate 6. Powell's Forest, Buckhurst Hill, where George Burney and his 'gang' pulled down fences in January 1878.

Plate 7. Title page of the Minute Book 1866–69, of the Commons Preservation Society, East of London Committee.

Plate 8. Memorandum from George Burney to Mrs Willingale, August 1880, indicating that he hopes to obtain a pension for her.

Plate 9. Advertisement for the Testimonial Lunch at the Forest Hotel, 1880.

Plate 10. Burney Pamphlet for his evidence to the Arbitrator in 1879.

Plate 11. Plan for the Queen's Park Estate, Loughton, sold in March 1886.

Acknowledgements

THE photograph of the silver *épergne* presented to George Burney in 1880, is reproduced by permission of the London Borough of Redbridge. The plan of the wharves on the Mellish estate, Isle of Dogs in 1893, is reproduced from the *Survey of London*, vol. XLIII, 1994, by permission of English Heritage. The image of the title page of the Minute Book of the East of London Committee of the Commons Preservation Society is reproduced by permission of the London Borough of Tower Hamlets Archives. The title page of George Burney's address at the proceedings of the Arbitrator is reproduced by permission of Guildhall Library, City of London Corporation. I am grateful to the archivists of the London Boroughs of Tower Hamlets and Newham Archives, and at the London Metropolitan Archives and Guildhall Library, for their assistance in the research for this monograph, and to Stan Newens, Mark Gorman, Sophie Lillington and Catherine Cavanagh for their interest in the project.

I am most grateful to Ted Martin for his invaluable help in preparing the book for the press.

RM

Introduction

GEORGE BURNEY, an iron-tank manufacturer from Millwall on the Isle of Dogs in East London, achieved some notoriety in the 1870s, in the fight to save Epping Forest from enclosure, when he organised the pulling down of fences on pieces of forest land which he believed had been illegally enclosed. His involvement in helping to save the Forest was, however, much greater than just pulling down fences. This monograph seeks to explain his wider activities in this respect, and to give some background to his family and business in east London. Burney & Company Ltd became known internationally for its iron products and was sole supplier of iron water tanks to the Royal Navy.

Early life

GEORGE BURNEY was the elder son of John and Mary Ann Burney. He was born at Glass House Yard in the parish of Aldgate, on 13 September 1818. The occupation of his father is shown as 'Tide Waiter' (Customs Inspector). George had a brother, William, born in 1822, and five sisters: Jane (b. 1819), Catherine (b. 1824), Mary Ann (b. 1826), Ellen (b. 1828), and Sarah (b. 1829). The parish register states that Catherine was 'born at sea'. All seven children were somewhat unusually baptised on the same day, 26 December 1830, at the church of St George-in-the-East, Stepney, when George would have been in his twelfth year. George Burney appears to have lived at Bow in Tower Hamlets from an early age.

References by Burney to his first interest in Epping Forest appear in the records of evidence he gave when opposing enclosures in the Forest, and show that he started to visit the Forest for recreation by the time he was nine years of age in 1828. We have no record of George's education, but he was in business as an iron tank manufacturer at the age of 30 if not earlier.

There is no evidence that George Burney inherited any great wealth, and he appears to have become a successful businessman through his own efforts although, in his early career, in partnership with Edward Bellamy.

George took an active part in his local community in Poplar, and was concerned about unemployment and living conditions in and around the Millwall area, with many people on poor relief. As with Epping Forest, Burney was forthright in expressing his views on these social problems and trying to do something about them.

In 1868 it was proposed to build a new permanent church of St Luke's at Millwall (until then there had only been a small iron church). Apart from the need for a larger church, the decision to construct a brick built one, would provide much needed work for the unemployed – carpenters, bricklayers and general labourers.

The proposal was published in local newspapers with a call for donations. George Burney was a member of the fund-raising committee, and was one of the early contributors when he gave £100. The church was consecrated in 1870, but St Luke's was damaged in the Second World War and demolished in 1960.

Marriage

BURNEY married twice. First he married Harriet (maiden name not known but born in 1801). The date of the marriage has not yet been found but we can deduce from the 1851 Census that Harriet was 18 years older than George and died before 1854. No children appear to have been born of this marriage.

George Burney's second marriage was to Mary Spencer, at the church of St John of Jerusalem in South Hackney, on 20 June 1854. A special licence was required from the Bishop as Mary was a minor of 17 years. George was by then 35. Mary was the daughter of James Spencer, who appears on the marriage register as a 'Treenail maker' (a maker of special copper nails or wooden pegs for shipbuilding). He was a widower by the time of his daughter's marriage and came to live with George and Mary. Mary Ann Burney is shown as a witness to the marriage, who could have been either his mother or sister. George is stated to be a widower (following the death of Harriet). By 1861 George and Mary were living at 79 Stainsby Road, Poplar, just south of the Limehouse Cut. As we shall see only the first of their children had been born by then, although George, Mary, and her father James Spencer, had two servants living with them, which suggests that the tank manufacturing business was profitable.

Children

GEORGE AND MARY BURNEY had two sons, George and Herman, and two daughters, Eleanor and Mabel.

The first child to be born was George Spencer Burney who was baptised on 14 July 1858 at the church of St John of Jerusalem in South Hackney. The family were living at Stainsby Road at this time. However, George Spencer Burney died early in 1860 at the age of 18 months. In his evidence to the Select Committee on Royal Forests (Essex) in 1863, George Burney makes reference to a child buried in the City of London Cemetery, at Manor Park, and this is likely to have been his son, George Spencer Burney.

Herman was the next child to be born, in April 1862, and he was also baptised at the church of St John of Jerusalem. He attended King's College School in London before going on to Trinity College, Cambridge in 1881. Herman probably read law and received a BA degree in 1884. In the same year he was admitted to Lincoln's Inn and was called to the Bar in 1888. The 1891 census finds him in Charlton Kings, Cheltenham, Gloucestershire, apparently as a partner in a brewery firm: C K Brewery. He was living with W R Wire, his business partner, and Susannah Spencer, a widow aged 63, is shown as the housekeeper. She may have been related to Mary Burney's family. The 1901 census, however, shows that Herman had returned to Greenwich and was living with his mother and two sisters. His occupation is now described as Barrister/solicitor.

Five years later Herman married Violet Canton at Emmanuel Church, Hampstead. They do not appear to have had any children, and by 1911 they were living in Reading, where Herman was Secretary to the Royal Berkshire Hospital. In retirement Herman moved to Poole, Dorset where he died in May 1938, aged 76.

Eleanor was born in 1865, and was baptised at the church of St John of Jerusalem on 5 May. The church register shows that George and Mary were living at Blenheim House, Bow at this time. Eleanor does not appear to have married – she was living with her widowed mother, Mary, at Poole, Dorset, in 1911, at the age of 46 years, and was still a spinster at the time her brother made his will in 1935.

The 1871 census shows that the Burney family had moved across the river to Greenwich and were living at 26 Crooms Hill. Mary's father was still living with them, and by now three servants including a cook, nurse, and a housemaid were part of the household.

The younger daughter, Mabel, was born in 1874. She first married Ernest Biss in 1906, but he had died by 1911, and in 1914 she married Charles Steel. At that time Mabel was living with her mother, Mary Burney, at Glensdale, Poole, Dorset. Mabel died in July 1927.

Burney & Company Ltd

GEORGE BURNEY and Edward Bellamy acquired premises at 118 Westferry Road, on the Isle of Dogs, Poplar, in about 1850. Originally the firm made iron water-tanks for ships, becoming the sole makers for the Royal Navy. Patents were obtained for various types of tank lids and flanges.

In 1881 they employed 120 people. By the end of the century they were producing a wide range of galvanized or painted sheet-metal, cast-iron, wire and brass products, including cisterns, hoppers, barrows, cattle-troughs, guttering, ventilators and cowls, boilers, plumbing fittings and netting. The firm ceased trading in 1932. Much of the factory's output was exported, and they were well known in Australia.

The tank-works buildings, which were a mixture of corrugated-iron and brick construction, were damaged by bombing in the Second World War, and in 1943 the cleared site was taken over by the wharfingers at Timothy's Wharf next door and used for storage of chemicals. After the war it was merged with Timothy's and Mellish's Wharves to form Arnhem Wharf.

Burney also took over the disused Walker's Iron Works on the corner of Tiller Road (formerly Glengall Grove) and Westferry Road in about 1860. A plan of 1893-94 shows a Burney factory on the west side of Westferry Road with a frontage on to the river, but this may be the original site referred to above.

The Fight to Save Epping Forest

AS WE HAVE SEEN, Burney was brought up in East London, and made regular visits to Epping Forest in his younger years. In 1863, he gave evidence to the Select Committee on Royal Forests (Essex), in which he said that he had 'enjoyed the uninterrupted privilege of the use of that [Epping] forest for 35 years; as far back, or nearly so, as I can recollect'. This would have made him nine years old when he first visited Epping Forest. Burney also gave evidence during the hearings of the Arbitrator in 1879, into enclosure of 68 acres of forest waste made by Peter Gellatly in Loughton manor. In an eloquent speech Burney said 'the fact is that forty years ago [1839] I used to go and recreate myself in the blackberry orchards . . . of the manor, and on this very land which is now withheld by Mr Gellatly's illegal fence, and I must say that I had a wonderful deal more enjoyment and recreation upon that ground than I have now. . .'

Protests against enclosures

Burney appeared before the Select Committee on Royal Forests (Essex) on 7 May 1863. He gave his address as Blenheim House, Bow, and his profession as a tank manufacturer. He commented that his use of the Forest over the previous 10 or 12 years had been very much interfered with by encroachments that threatened almost the absorption of the Forest. He emphasised the importance of the Forest to the people of east London as it was within walking distance for many of them – only three miles from Bow where he lived.

It is interesting that at this stage in his support for the fight against enclosures, he was not against all enclosures, and admitted that there were some portions of the Forest which might be enclosed without detriment to anybody, except probably to Commoners who have rights of pasturage over it. He admitted to the Chairman of the Committee that he was not acquainted with the rights of the soil or of the Commoners, and that he represented only the popular feeling with regard to the exercise and air that people obtained from the Forest. Burney was to later acquire some land in Loughton which gave him Commoners' rights, after which he changed his mind and objected to any enclosures.

William Whitaker Maitland, the lord of the manor of Loughton, had purchased the forestal rights of his manor from the Crown in 1860, and started selling plots of land to local people. Three hundred acres had been sold during the next five years, when his son, the Rev John Whitaker Maitland, who had become lord of the manor, started to enclose the remaining 900 acres of the forest waste in his manor. This action led to protests by the villagers against the loss of their lopping rights and Thomas Willingale, with financial support from some well known residents, initiated legal proceedings in 1866 against the lord of the manor. George Burney came to know the Willingale family and benefited from their knowledge of the forest. He was later to assist in obtaining a pension for Mrs Willingale from the City of London Corporation.

The Metropolitan Board of Works

In 1864, following the recommendations of the Select Committee on Royal Forests (Essex), the Government approached the Metropolitan Board of Works and asked if they would be interested in acquiring the forestal rights of the Crown for the remaining part of Epping Forest where the rights had not been sold to the local lords of the manor. This proposal came to the attention of George Burney and in July 1864 he wrote to the Metropolitan Board of Works:

'Noticing that the control of this valuable public right is offered you, I beg to inform you that a Deputation of influential persons desire to wait upon you, to urge your acceptance of this trust, and to offer co-operation, if desired, by those persons, who have already studied the question.'

While the proposal may have been seen by Burney to guarantee the right of the public to roam throughout the then remaining 3,000 acres of the Forest, it offered little to the MBW, as the lords of the manor would still own the soil and other manorial rights. It did not of course address the 1,800 acres that had already been sold and enclosed.

Discussions continued intermittently between the Government and the MBW over the next six years, and were further complicated by other proposals including limiting public access for recreation to an area of only 600 acres. George Burney's only other reference to the Metropolitan Board of Works came in 1878, when he suggested that they should be represented on the City of London Corporation management committee of the Forest, but his proposal was not taken up.

The Commons Preservation Society – East of London Local Committee

In July 1865 the Commons Preservation Society had been formed under the leadership of George Shaw-Lefevre (later Lord Eversley) with the object of organising resistance to the threatened enclosure of Commons in the neighbourhood of London.

Matters were moving quickly with the purchase by the lords of the manor of the forestal rights of the Crown, and the subsequent sale of over 700 acres of Epping Forest to local landowners who promptly put up fences around the plots. This caused great indignation in the east of London whose people had enjoyed the Forest for recreation, and by February 1866, an 'East of London Local Committee', of the Commons Preservation Society had been formed. A committee meeting was held at the Royal Hotel in the Mile End Road on Saturday, 10 February, which was attended by Andrew Johnston, Gilbert Marshall, Donald Munro and George Burney. Edward North Buxton was elected a member of the Committee, and a representative of the Metropolitan Board of Works gave his ideas on the question of saving Epping Forest from enclosure.

The Minute Book of the East London Committee for the period 1866–69 has survived and shows that the Committee met every week, organised public meetings, prepared circulars on the subject of enclosure, and sought subscriptions for membership of the local branch of the Society. At a public meeting held at the Beaumont Institute at Beaumont Square, Stepney, George Burney proposed:

'That legal advice be taken to ascertain the right of lords of the manor to enclose the waste lands within the Forest, and that the committee be authorised to adopt measures to resist illegal enclosures, and to protect the public and local interests in the enjoyment of the Forest as they may think expedient; and this meeting pledges itself to use its influence to invite subscriptions with a view to raise a fund of £10,000 to defray the necessary expenses of such measures'.

Burney thought that the funds might be raised by 100 persons binding themselves for £100 each, and he should be most happy to put himself down as one of the list.

We first come across Burney in the Forest at a protest meeting organised by the East of London Committee on 22 April 1867. The open air meeting was held opposite the King's Oak Tavern, High Beach,

Loughton, on Easter Monday, when the annual stag hunt took place, with many thousands of pleasure-seekers assembled in the Forest, and a report of the meeting appeared in *The Times* on 23 April.

The chairman of the meeting was Mr Duffield of Mile End, who briefly explained the objects of the association, and called upon the inhabitants of the district to support it. If they suffered the encroachment which had commenced to go on, it would not be long before the whole of Epping Forest would be enclosed, and the crowded population of the eastern district of the metropolis deprived of the valuable means of recreation which they now enjoyed.

George Burney, in moving a resolution pledging the meeting to co-operate in resisting the enclosure of the Forest said:

'It was a fact that upwards of 6,000 children had been brought down from London in one day to enjoy themselves in the Forest, and it was anything but patriotic on the part of the Rev. Mr Maitland, the lord of the manor, to attempt to enclose it. The rev. gentleman had, it appeared, purchased 1,400 acres from the Crown Commissioners at £100* per acre and £4 10s. per acre for Crown Rights, and this land he had enclosed.'

[*These figures appear confused. A Schedule prepared by the Office of Woods in 1862 quotes £5,468 being paid to the Crown for 1,377 acres in the manor of Loughton, which would give a price per acre of just under £4. When the City of London purchased the forest waste from Maitland in 1876, they paid £20 per acre.]

Burney continued:

'Now, if any of this land was sold for building purposes it would fetch about £1,000 per acre. He contended that the whole affair was illegal, because the rights of the people had not been considered, and they could not be bartered away. They were not worthy of the name of Englishmen if they did not resist this oppression by every means in their power. A considerable amount had been subscribed and the society was determined to try the issue by legal means if necessary. It was not only the rich that had rights – the poor had rights also, and if the rich put up fences where they had no right to do so, the poor would be justified in pulling them down again.'

It is interesting to note that Burney was already contemplating the possibility of pulling fences down, although in reply to a question at the meeting, it was stated that the committee did not advise such action at present, until some legal steps had been taken.

A similar meeting took place at Chingford Green in July, which was attended by Charles Watkins of Queen Elizabeth's Lodge, Purlieu Ranger, who stated that he considered the farmers were unfairly shut out of their [common] rights of pasturage, as only about 50 acres remained unenclosed out of 300 in Mr Hodgson's manor.

An interesting note is added in the Minute Book of the East London Committee in August 1867, which states that it was 'agreed that all guarantees to the funds of the East London Committee be transferred to the Epping Forest Preservation Society upon their undertaking the liabilities and to carry out the objectives of this Committee'. Why this change took place is a little difficult to understand. The minutes of meetings tend to suggest some difficulties between some of the leading members of the Committee, but the meetings and lobbying against enclosures continued, and by now the Government was under pressure to do something.

The Epping Forest Preservation Society

In September 1867, the East London Committee of the Commons Preservation Society became the Epping Forest Preservation Society and Burney was elected its Chairman. A notice was inserted in local newspapers advising readers of the change of name and earnestly inviting:

'the co-operation and aid of all classes of the people to enable them to rescue these public lands from the illegal enclosures of private individuals, and secure them for the use and enjoyment of the people for ever.'

In the autumn an excursion of members and friends was made to Loughton and back, by road and rail. An impression had somehow got abroad that the object of the excursion was to throw down the palings that had been erected by Mr Maitland, and large numbers of persons were eager to attend for that purpose. But the idea of violence being steadily discountenanced by the Society, none attended but those who were willing simply to view the enclosures.

The excursionists having roamed about to their hearts' content through the gates of the enclosed lands (which, while the suits in Chancery continued, could not be closed) met in the afternoon on the hill by the side of the new Schools. Resolutions were passed in support of the actions of the two Societies. A newspaper report concluded that:

'Some apprehension appears to have been entertained by the authorities lest the excursionists should be maltreated by the inhabitants, as a large body of police, both horse and foot, were sent down for their protection. It is pleasing, therefore, to be able to state that the Cockneys were received by the natives with the greatest possible kindness. The day was, therefore, spent by the police, as by everybody else, in the happiest possible manner.'

By July 1869, a public meeting chaired by E R Cook, expressed satisfaction with the determination expressed by the Government to preserve Epping Forest as an open space for the use of the people of London, and to take legal proceedings against those unauthorised persons who had illegally enclosed portions of Epping Forest. There is no further surviving record of the Committee's meetings, but of course, as we shall see, George Burney continued his own crusade.

Parliament and the Courts become involved

The pressure exerted by the Commons Preservation Society and its members in Parliament led the Government to introduce a Bill in July 1871, which became the Epping Forest Act of 1871, under which commissioners were appointed to report on the enclosures and encroachments and to prepare a scheme for disafforestation, that is Epping Forest would cease to be a royal forest, and how the Forest would be managed in the future.

In the same month that the Act of 1871 came into force, the City of London Corporation filed a Bill in Chancery on 14 August 1871, against the Lords of the Manors in Epping Forest, who had made enclosures on the forest waste, claiming that the Commoners' (of which the City Corporation was one) right to graze their cattle over the length and breadth of the Forest had been restricted by the enclosures, and they were therefore illegal.

It was to take until 1874 for judgment to be given by the Master of the Rolls in this action, and the Epping Forest Commissioners were to take evidence for over five years before their Final Report was published. Throughout this time protest meetings against the enclosures continued to be held in Town Halls in East London and on the Forest itself. The Forest Fund was founded in 1871, following a protest meeting on Wanstead Flats, and joined the Commons Preservation Society and the City of London Corporation in the forefront of the fight to save the Forest.

Direct action

In George Burney's view all the illegal fences should have come down immediately after the judgment of the Master of the Rolls in November 1874, but the Epping Forest Commissioners were still to issue their final report with a proposed scheme for disafforestation and management of the Forest in the future. The matter became further complicated when the Commissioners' scheme proposed that grants of forest waste made since 1851 should be allowed to remain enclosed (other than those in the possession of the lords of manors).

In Loughton some well known persons such as John Chilton and Peter Gellatly had purchased plots from William Whitaker Maitand and enclosed them with fences; Nathanael Powell in Buckhurst Hill had similarly enclosed a tract of land on the west side of the hill from the cricket ground down to Manor Road, and Mr G Borwick had erected over a mile of fencing around land at Wanstead that he had purchased from Lord Cowley. In January 1878, Burney decided to take direct action, one of the results of which was that the Epping Forest Act of 1878 provided that an Arbitrator would decide which enclosures would have to be returned to the Forest.

Burney published and circulated the following Notice:

PUBLIC NOTICE

I, GEORGE BURNEY of Mill Wall, Poplar, Chairman of the Epping Forest Preservation Society and Commoner of Loughton hereby announce that by the decision of the Master of the Rolls certain Lands in Epping Forest were found to be illegally enclosed. A portion of these Lands were in consequence of such decision thrown open by the City Authorities; but they or other Commoners have failed to remove the illegal Fences enclosing about 760 Acres, and such Fences remain to the damage of the Commoners and great injury of the natural beauty of the Forest.

It is not proposed in any arrangement that the interests of the Commoners are to be taken into account, and if such Lands remain enclosed it will be to the permanent injury and restriction of the Commoners' rights, and such enclosures are in defiance of justice and in contempt of the law as so decided by the Master of the Rolls.

I therefore as a Commoner in vindication of the law and in support of my rights have instructed the said illegal Fences to be removed, and declare all the said Lands to be and to remain open for the use of the Commoners, Owners and Occupiers according to their respective rights for ever. Any persons attempting to reinstate such Fences will be liable to an Action by any Commoner.

Persons not having rights are cautioned not to interfere and all persons are warned that although the said Fences are pulled down they remain the Property of those who put them up. Persons having Crops or Property of any sort in the illegal enclosures are warned to remove them so as to avoid damage by the Commoners' Cattle.

Signed
GEORGE BURNEY

On the morning of 16 January 1878, Burney with a large crowd of workmen acting under his orders, arrived in several open carriages at Wanstead and demolished the 'illegal' fences, before proceeding to Buckhurst Hill and Loughton to do the same. A lengthy report of the events of the day appeared in the *Stratford Express* on 19 January:

'DESTROYING FENCES ON THE FOREST LAND
On Wednesday last [16 January] a great deal of excitement was caused in this neighbourhood, Wanstead, at Buckhurst Hill and Loughton, by the destruction of fences on enclosed forest land. Soon after ten o'clock on the morning of the day named four handsome private 'busses, each drawn by four magnificent grey horses, preceded by a handsome carriage drawn by greys, appeared in Cambridge Park-road, Wanstead. The 'busses were loaded with decently-dressed labourers and mechanics, according to appearances, and each 'bus contained some five and twenty men, making altogether a hundred stalwart fellows, who appeared active and willing enough to execute anything they were called upon to perform. Arriving at this spot, a stop was made, and the men alighted. It was not long before a good sprinkling of spectators gathered together. The men had with them a curious assortment of tools, evidently new, including saws, axes, hammers, pickaxes, crowbars, and ropes, and it was evident that there was some mischief in the wind.

The leader of the party having noticed PC Welthey on duty near the spot, called his attention to the fact that he that day and henceforth and for evermore declared that portion of the forest free and open to the public, and after giving his name as George Burney, of Millwall, and saying that he acted according to the decree of the Master of the Rolls, he marshalled his men into three gangs, and the work of destroying the fencing on the land of Mr Borwick commenced. The land in question contains many acres, and we believe was bought by Mr Borwick of Lord Cowley for a sum of £20,000. It is bounded by the Cambridge Park-road, Park-road, and Ilford-road, and the fencing altogether was about a mile in length.

In a few minutes over a half-an-hour every rail had been levelled to the ground, so expertly did the gangs perform their allotted tasks. They once more assembled their tools, put them together, and mounting their vehicles, gave three cheers for the 'open forest', and proceeded in the direction of Woodford. They again commenced their work of devastation at Buckhurst Hill on enclosed land in the occupation of N Powell Esq., JP. About half a mile of fencing soon shared the same fate as that at Wanstead, and with quite as much dispatch. Crossing the road they next attacked the fencing surrounding land in the occupation of Mr Gellatly, of Loughton, and at least a mile of woodwork was levelled with the ground and completed in the same workmanlike manner, amidst the cheers of the men when the work was completed, they at the same time behaving in the most decorous manner as heretofore.

This work having been completed they adjourned to the Crown, at Loughton, where they partook of luncheon and made themselves most comfortable. Previous to this, however, we may mention that they demolished a gate belonging to the nursery of Mr Paul, of Waltham Cross, and entering the nursery, Mr Burney, addressing those assembled, declared the Forest free and open to the public that day and for evermore. After leaving the 'Crown', they proceeded to a fence between there and the New Woodford-road, and upon land belonging to Mr Abbot, which they speedily demolished. From there they went to the left in the direction of London, and next demolished a most substantial fence belonging to Mr John Chilton, of the Robin Hood. This seems to have been the completion of their work, and once more assembling in their vehicles, made their way home in the same good order as when they commenced their work. They stopped at the 'Green Man' at Leytonstone for refreshment, and here indulged in a little banter as to the 'good work' they had completed. As soon as they commenced operations Inspector Anderson was quickly in the saddle, and together with Sergt. Hughes, was shortly in company with the devastators, but did not stop them or interfere with them. Later on they were joined by the Superintendent of the district, Mr Green, together with Inspector Todman, and other constables, and they contented themselves with learning the names of the principal parties concerned, and in seeing that no breach of the peace occurred. The amount of damage is estimated at £2,000.'

The same issue of *The Stratford Express* included a short leader on the subject:

'Mr George Burney has taken upon himself to assert the rights of the Epping Forest Commoners and the majesty of the law by the demolition of some miles of fencing on the Forest. This eccentric proceeding may in the eyes of some be a good joke, while others will look upon it as a wilful destruction of property not to be tolerated. Another pretty little lawsuit is the most probable result of the business, and the cause of the 'Forest for the People' is not likely to gain much of it. However, it is just one more illustration of the necessity of finally settling the vexed question, and although, when it is settled unanimity of opinion is not likely to be the effect, it would at any rate prevent the possibility of the repetition of an act which might have resulted in a serious riot.'

It is interesting that the 'Forest Fund Committee' wrote to some newspapers at this time stating that 'Mr Burney is not, and has never been, in any way connected with them'. The Forest Fund Committee was by 1878 in close contact with the Epping Forest Commissioners and Parliament in drafting the Epping Forest Act, and probably did not wish to be seen to condone an illegal act.

Court cases

John Chilton, the landlord of the Robin Hood Inn, Nathanael Powell, and Mr Borwick from Wanstead, applied to the High Court to seek injunctions restraining Burney from any repetition of pulling fences down and also claimed damages.

Powell and Borwick's cases (together with another plaintiff: Mr Venables) were heard in the High Court on 25 January, before the Master of the Rolls, a report of which appeared in *The Times*:

HIGH COURT OF JUSTICE, Jan 25
CHANCERY DIVISION
(*Before the* MASTER *of the* ROLLS)

POWELL v. BURNEY; VENABLES v. BURNEY;
BORWICK v. BURNEY

These were motions in three actions to restrain the defendants from pulling down fences, injuring the growing of crops, and from committing or inciting any person to commit any waste or trespass upon certain enclosed lands, now in the occupation of the respective plaintiffs, situated within Epping Forest, and mentioned in the schedule to the final report of the Epping Forest Commissioners, and from preventing the plaintiffs from reinstating any fences which have been pulled down until the end of the present Session of Parliament. The respective plaintiffs are owners of enclosures of waste land in the Forest, which are found by such final report to have been illegally made as against the persons entitled to rights of common. In the Commissioners' scheme, made in pursuance of the Epping Forest Act of 1871, for the disafforestation and preservation of the Forest, and now before Parliament for confirmation, they recommend that all persons, other than lords of manors in possession of illegal enclosure shall be allowed to remain in possession thereof, paying to the future governing body of the Forest nine-tenths of the agricultural value of the land.

The defendant, Mr George Burney, is the owner of a house in the parish of Loughton, and is entitled in respect thereof to certain rights of common, under the decree of the Master of the Rolls, made in the suit of the *Commissioners of Sewers* v. *Glasse*. Mr Burney appeared by counsel before the Commissioners and objected to the above provision in their report, but his objections were overruled by them. He recently, to assert his common rights which he alleged would be interfered with if the scheme were sanctioned, caused a gang of men to pull down over two miles of fencing round the plaintiffs' enclosures.

The Master of the Rolls said the defendant alleged that he only desired to try the question of right, but to do that it was clearly unnecessary to pull down some two miles of fencing and to do damage to the extent of about £100. That looked like wanton mischief and influenced him to some extent in granting the injunction. His lordship then granted an injunction in each action in terms of the respective notices of motion, without prejudice to any question in the action, the costs being reserved.

In Powell's case a further hearing before the Master of the Rolls took place on 24 May, 1878, to settle the question of the defendant's (Burney's) counterclaim. A report of this hearing also appeared in *The Times*:

HIGH COURT OF JUSTICE, May 24
CHANCERY DIVISION
(*Before the* MASTER *of the* ROLLS)

POWELL v. BURNEY

This was a motion on behalf of the plaintiffs to strike out the defendant's counter-claim, on the ground that he had not obtained the sanction of the Epping Forest Commissioners to bring the same under section 3 of the Epping Forest Act of 1872. The plaintiffs allege that they are owners in fee of certain enclosed lands in the Forest, but on the 16 January 1878, the defendant, who claims rights of common over these lands, with a number of workmen and others entered thereon, and pulled down about two miles of fences enclosing the same, and doing considerable damage. The plaintiffs then commenced this action by leave of the Epping Forest Commissioners, and obtained an injunction restraining the defendant from further sets of trespass until the trial. In addition to his statement of defence the defendant had put in a counter-claim, claiming a declaration that he was entitled to rights of common over the waste, and an injunction to restrain the plaintiffs from interfering with the defendant's exercise of those rights.

Mr Chitty, QC, and Mr Vaughan Hawkins appeared for the plaintiffs; Mr Bagshawe, QC, and Mr W R Fisher for the defendant.

The MASTER of the ROLLS said there had been a vast litigation as to these common rights, which had culminated in the case of the *Commissioners of Sewers* v. *Glasse*. It was feared that further litigation might ensue, and therefore, the Legislature had taken the matter up, and had appointed certain Commissioners to inquire into and report on those rights, and had provided, in effect, that there should be no litigation in respect of them until the end of the session next, after they had made such report except by consent of the Commissioners. The defendant had endeavoured to get over this provision by a side-wind by compelling an action to be brought by the plaintiffs with consent, and then to obtain all he wanted by a counter-claim without such consent. The counter-claim was, in his opinion, practically new litigation, and within the mischief intended to be prevented. He should, therefore, order the counter-claim to be struck out, with costs.

Burney may have lost the day, but the final outcome was left to the Arbitrator, to decide which enclosures had to be thrown back into the Forest. Burney gave evidence at the proceedings before the Arbitrator in the *Paul's*, *Gellatly* and *Borwick* cases.

A Commoner in Loughton

George Burney purchased a small estate in Loughton including a house in York Hill, with the object of acquiring Commoners' rights in Epping Forest. The land that he purchased was between York Hill, Pump Hill (formerly Lyngs Lane) and Church Hill. Waller, in his *History of Loughton*, refers to this as 'Home Mead', and possibly 'Blacksmiths Field', in total 14 acres, but does not give a date for the purchase. In 1881 Jesse Wakelin was the tenant living at the house (Tilekiln Farm) in York Hill. Burney also acquired a property at the southern end of the High Road, in Victoria Place, which adjoined Nafferton Lodge on the west side of the High Road. In 1881 the property was let to William Doyley the well known Loughton surveyor.

The estate at the northern end of the village was sold and broken up for building in 1886 following George Burney's death, and became the Queen's Park estate.

In 1881 Burney was appointed one of the first six Trustees of the Lopping Endowment (the initial Trustees were replaced a year later when the Trustees were elected by the ratepayers of Loughton) the principal object of which was to erect buildings suitable for the purposes of a Reading and Lecture Room and as a place of meeting for parochial purposes. The Endowment was funded from the compensation awarded by the Arbitrator for the loss of lopping rights.

Burney pamphlets

George Burney published at least seven pamphlets between 1870 and 1880. They all concerned aspects of the fight to save Epping Forest from enclosure and the rights of the villagers in the forest parishes.

The first pamphlet to be published has the title *Epping Forest to be Saved at Last: The various Rights examined, and the Sales made shown to be Illegal*, and although it has no date was probably published in 1870 or early 1871. The pamphlet runs to over thirty pages and has three sections.

In the first section Burney endeavours to provide a plain review of the whole question of the future of the Forest, and identifies four issues to be argued:
1. The Rights of Lords of Manors and Commoners.
2. The Sale of Crown Rights, extending over Manors, illegal by reason of existing law, and the absence of a special Act of Parliament.
3. While the reigning Sovereign receives the Civil List the Rights of the Crown absolutely belong to the People.
4. The means of preserving the Forest cheaply and effectually.

The second section of the pamphlet consists of the Minutes of a meeting held with the Chancellor of the Exchequer in August 1869. Following a public meeting of the inhabitants of Mile-End Old Town, a deputation visited the Chancellor, led by Mr Samuda, MP, together with three other MPs, and eleven local inhabitants including George Burney. Two representatives from the Commons Preservation Society were also in attendance. A Memorial was presented to the Chancellor and a vigorous debate followed as to what rights the Crown and the Lords of the Manors each had in the ownership of the Forest. The deputation proposed that the Crown should restore its old forestal rights to prevent encroachments on Epping Forest, and to preserve it for the benefit of the public. Mr Lowe, the Chancellor, admitted the importance of the object, but he objected to the means proposed of securing it.

The arguments put forward by George Burney and his colleagues and the Chancellor's response formed the basis of an article in the *Spectator* on 7 August 1869, and the article is reprinted in the third section of the pamphlet.

The proposals put forward for the protection of Epping Forest fell well wide of the final outcome eight years later, but some of the principles and facts laid down in the pamphlet formed a basis for the ensuing debate.

In February 1872, George Burney published a pamphlet under the title *Epping Forest to be Saved Without a Corn Tax*! While recognising that some progress had been made by the Epping Forest Act of 1871, which appointed Commissioners to inquire into the rights and claims of the Forest and to prepare a scheme for the disafforestation of Epping Forest and for its preservation and management, Burney was still concerned with some proposals included in a further Bill which the Government had tabled.

The pamphlet emphasised that the public must be unanimous in demanding that the 'whole 5,000 acres are to be preserved for their [public] use. The money received [by the Crown] for the illegal sales [of the forestal rights] must be paid back, with any moderate compensation that justice requires'. Any encroachment on which houses had been built could remain subject to the payment of a fine.

Burney put forward his own proposal for the saving of Epping Forest 'without taxation of the food [the corn tax] of the people – or any other kind'. He estimated that an endowment of £100,000 was needed to provide sufficient income for the management of the Forest, which he considered 'a mere fleabite'.

It was December 1876 before Burney went into print again, although during the intervening years he was very active in both the protest and lobbying activities of the day. His new pamphlet had the title *The Present State of the Epping Forest Question*, and was dedicated to the Hon W Cowper Temple MP. The Epping Forest Commissioners had a year earlier issued their draft Report containing proposals for the future of the Forest. Burney's pamphlet was a critique of the proposals which he submitted to the Commissioners. In February 1877 the Commissioners issued their Final Report.

Within three months Burney published another pamphlet, under the same title but dated May 1877, containing his views on the Final Report. He commented first on the improvements made since the Commissioners' draft Report, but states that 'plenty of *bad* remains'. The first criticism is that 'representation [on the management committee] is utterly denied to the immense populations who are certainly not represented either by the City or the Verderers'. However, Burney continues that

'The greatest blot of the whole scheme is that 760 acres of forest land, distinct and in addition to a liberal allowance for curtilage to houses, are either to be retained by the present illegal holders at a puerile fine, or else bought back by the City at the value of building land.'

As we have seen Burney was to use both lobbying and direct action to force Parliament to think again before including the latter proposal in the Epping Forest Bill. He was also ready to co-operate with public bodies and individuals in seeking their representation in the management of the Forest, but in this he failed.

Reference has already been made to the evidence that George Burney gave to the proceedings before the Arbitrator in the cases which had earlier involved him in legal actions. His evidence was subsequently published in a pamphlet under the title *Epping Forest, Proceedings Before the Arbitrator, Sir A Hobhouse, Address of Mr Burney, 19th June, and 21st & 22nd July 1879, Paul's Case, Gellatly and Borwick's Cases*.

Burney was to go into print on one more occasion when he published a brief one-page pamphlet with the title *The Lopping Rights in Loughton*. No publication date is shown, but could have been about 1880, and refers to 'the decision of the Arbitrator confirming the Rights of Lopping to the inhabitants of Loughton, which rights, I need hardly observe, are very valuable to all classes of inhabitants'. Within a very short time the Arbitrator had agreed a scheme under which the inhabitants of Loughton lost their lopping rights and received compensation.

Recognition

ON Saturday 12 June 1880, some 300 people sat down to a public luncheon in a large pavilion erected on the lawn of the Forest Hotel at Chingford.

Tickets cost 6s. or Double Tickets (Lady and Gentleman), 10s., and Sir Antonio Brady, JP, FGS, Verderer, was in the Chair. The purpose of the lunch was the presentation of Testimonials and Addresses to Sir Thomas Nelson, Lieut-Col Palmer, J T Bedford, Esq, W G S Smith Esq, E J Daniell Esq, and George Burney, for services which had in various ways greatly helped to preserve about 6,000 acres of Epping Forest for the use of the people.

All the recipients of the honours were present, with the exception of Colonel Palmer, who was too old and infirm to attend, and who was represented by his son. Colonel Palmer received a large silver tray-beautifully chased in the Italian style.

Mr Deputy Bedford and George Burney were each presented with a handsome silver épergne representing forest scenery and deer.

Burney's épergne was engraved with the following inscription:

PRESENTED
To
George Burney Esq.
OF MILL WALL
by Public Subscription
as a recognition of his exertions
over TWENTY FIVE YEARS
in securing SIX THOUSAND ACRES
IN EPPING FOREST
For the use of the Public for ever
June 1880

In 1937 the épergne was given by his son, Herman, to the Borough of Wanstead and Woodford and was inherited by the London Borough of Redbridge, when the London Boroughs were created in 1964. (John Bedford's épergne is in the Corporation of London collection at the Mansion House.)

Mr W G Smith, besides a service of silver plate, received a valuable gold watch. Illuminated addresses were presented to Sir Thomas Nelson and Mr E J Daniell.

The presentation to George Burney had been arranged through a separate Testimonial Fund to which the public were invited to subscribe.

Burney had incurred legal costs of £1,369 18s 6d in defending in the High Court his actions in pulling down fences. He first raised the question of being compensated for these costs in 1879 when he had added an Addendum to his pamphlet on his evidence to the proceedings of the Arbitrator:

'There is a movement on foot for a testimonial in which my name is left out. As I have only worked twenty-five years and spent hundreds in money, and more in time, and taken thousands in responsibility, I beg to make a proposal. I don't want any testimonial, and therefore suggest that the money gathered might be well used in paying my costs. There would then be enough for a testimonial on vellum very handsomely got up, setting forth how long each one had worked in the good cause. I throw this out for public approval, especially as the wrongfully taken lands *are yet to be thrown open*. In the later years, no one has done more in my opinion than our sturdy Nelson of today – the City Solicitor [Thomas Nelson].

G BURNEY'

When the Epping Forest Arbitration awards were finally settled in 1882, there was £812 10s. left and from this Burney was given £650. Two years later, at a meeting of the Court of Common Council of the City of London Corporation on 24 April 1884, Deputy John Bedford presented a petition from George Burney asking the Court to recoup him the [balance of] expenses incurred by him in connection with the removal of illegal fences in Epping Forest, and the costs of the several actions brought against him in respect of such removal. The petition was referred to the Finance Committee for consideration and they recommended in October that he should be paid the balance of £719 18s. 6d.

Queen Victoria visited the Forest in May 1882, and George Burney was invited to the celebrations. It was somewhat ironic that his name on the list of guests was just four places below that of Peter Gellatly of Loughton, whose illegal fences on the Forest, Burney and his workmen had demolished four years earlier.

In the same year as the visit of Queen Victoria, George Burney received another presentation. This was a hatchet/axe which had the following inscription: 'Presented to Mr G Burney by the working men of East London in recognition of freeing Epping Forest, 1882.' At some later time, probably in 1937, the hatchet was given to the Borough of Wanstead & Woodford, and it resided in the Mayor's Parlour at the Borough's offices. Reference was made to the hatchet in 1946, by the then mayor of Wanstead and Woodford, Alderman F G Booth, but since then its whereabouts are unknown.

Death

BY 1881 the Burney family were living at 'The Limes', Greenwich. They had moved a few hundred yards up the hill from 26 Crooms Hill. When the census was taken in that year there were eleven people in the house: George, his wife (Mary) and their three children, Mary's father who was now 69 years old, Emily Binns a 'companion', Mary Armstrong a visitor, and three servants (a cook and two housemaids).

'The Limes' overlooked Greenwich Park and was a 'superior and spacious detached residence within its own walled-in grounds.' It had six bedrooms and dressing rooms, a spacious drawing room, dining and morning rooms, library, croquet lawn and flower gardens with a small greenhouse. The house was let on a full repairing lease for which George Burney paid £120 per annum. When the freehold was offered for sale in 1878, Burney was described in an advert as a 'highly responsible tenant'.

Burney was one of the early members of the Essex Field Club, which had been founded in 1880. Although his name does not appear in the Transactions of the Club, he gave financial support for its publications. In an obituary notice in 1885, the Club commented that Burney's direct action in January 1878, 'assuredly brought matters to a crisis, and helped, in a rough and ready way certainly, but with marked success, to the final settlement of a very difficult question'.

Throughout his life George Burney actively supported his local community and the City of London. In the 1860s the Poplar Hospital for Accidents held an annual 'festival' to raise funds. One event was a Dinner held at the Brunswick Hotel, Blackwall. Burney often acted as one of the stewards, and an advertisement for the Dinner in 1866, states that tickets cost one guinea and that 'Dinner to be on the table at 5 o'clock precisely'. The number of people at the Dinner must have been considerable as a special train was provided for guests returning to London.

In 1871 Burney received the Freedom of the City of London and in April of that year was admitted and sworn into the Freedom of the Gold and Silver Wyre Drawers' Livery Company.

George Burney died suddenly on 24 April 1885, in his 67th year. He was found dead in a train from Loughton on its arrival at Fenchurch Street Station. At a subsequent inquest, the verdict was that death was from 'effusion on the brain'. Burney was buried in Greenwich Cemetery on 29 April (although a grave number has been identified, its location appears to have been in an area now cleared of gravestones and monuments, and grassed over). An obituary in the *East London Observer* commented that:

'Mr Burney rendered great service to the East End of London in connection with the efforts to "save the Forest", and his plucky action in taking the law into his own hands to the extent of pulling down some obnoxious fences, brought about a decision which gave to the public a quantity of land which otherwise might have been enclosed until this day. He was the backbone of the old Epping Forest Committee [this probably refers to the Epping Forest Preservation Society Committee] which preceded the "Forest Fund Committee" [which was only founded in 1871], and all through his life did yeoman service. In recent years he did what lay in his power to promote Thames Communications. Though peculiar and even eccentric in manner, he was always to be relied upon for help in public matters; but he had a fault in that at times he manifested the John-Bull virtue of "pegging away", in such an exaggerated fashion as to approach a burlesque. Still he was ever a sound friend to all good movements, and will be much missed.'

Burney's interest in 'Thames Communications' referred to the possibility of a new tunnel east of London Bridge and two ferry services lower down the river.

The Notice of his death in *The Times* described him as of 'The Limes, Crooms Hill, Greenwich, and Millwall, London, E'.

When his will was proven this showed the gross value of his personal estate as £11,720. He had invested much of his wealth in property as can be seen from the advertisement in *The Standard* on 1 August 1885:

Re George Burney, Esq., deceased.
On Thursday 13th August, at one for two precisely.
MR BRADSHAW BROWN
will SELL by PUBLIC AUCTION,
at the Mart, Tokenhouse Yard, Lothbury E.C., the following properties:

GREENWICH, S.E.: Freehold Residence, No. 16 Crooms Hill, let to a yearly tenant at £40 per annum, tenant paying rates and taxes.

LOUGHTON: Copyhold Residence, Victoria Place, let on a three years' agreement at £32 per annum, tenant paying rates and taxes, held at a fine of 1½ years on death or alienation.

MILLWALL, E.: (In two Lots) Two Leasehold Dwelling houses with shops, Nos. 52 and 209 West Ferry Road, let on a lease of £50 and £37 10s per annum respectively, and held at a ground rent of £6. 10s and £2. 10s respectively, for an unexpired term of 58 years.

MILLWALL, E.: Leasehold Waterside Premises, known as Oak Wharf, let on lease at £120 per annum, held for an unexpired term of eleven years at £80 per annum.

BOW, E.: Eight Freehold Dwelling-houses, Nos. 1-8 Denbigh Terrace, Denbigh Road, let to weekly tenants, producing £204 per annum.

POPLAR, E.: Freehold Warehouse and Shop, No. 1 Pennyfields, West India Road, let on a lease at £30 per annum. And a Copyhold Dwelling-house with shop, No. 2 Pennyfields, let to a yearly tenant at £21 per annum, tenants paying rates and taxes.

OLD FORD, E.: Four Freehold Dwelling-houses, Nos. 433, 335 and 437 Old Ford Road, and 1 Autumn Street, producing £72. 8s per annum.

BROMLEY-BY-BOW: Seven Leasehold Dwelling-houses, Nos. 100 to 112 (even numbers) Bruce Road, let to weekly tenants, producing £143 per annum, held under long leases at £34 9s per annum. And Five Leasehold Dwelling-houses, Nos. 1–5 Railway cottages, Botolph Road, let to weekly tenants, producing £111 16s per annum. Held on long leases at a ground rent of £17. 15s per annum.

Solicitor, W Sturt Esq., 14 Ironmonger Lane, E.C.

Auctioneer's Offices: 59 Fenchurch Street, E.C. And Estate Offices: Millwall E.

In March 1886, the land which Burney acquired in Loughton in order to acquire Commoner status in Epping Forest was put up for sale at auction with building in mind:

'The FREEHOLD BUILDING ESTATE known as the Queen's Park Estate, Loughton, Essex, situate in a beautiful locality within 15 minutes' walk of Loughton Railway Station, and almost adjoining Epping Forest, having an area of about 15 acres, with a frontage to the high road from Loughton to Epping of 850ft.; the position and configuration of the property offer great advantages for profitable development, either by creation of ground-rents, resale in plots, or erection of moderate-sized villas, for which there is a ready demand.'

The estimated price quoted by the auctioneer was £2,800. A plan attached to details of the sale shows a proposed layout for the estate which included four roads. What today is Queen's Road was originally to be called Burney Road (see Plate 11), however, in the final plan prepared by the developer, the other three roads were omitted and Burney Road became Queen's Road.

Shortly after George Burney's death, Mary, his widow, her son Herman and the two daughters moved, from The Limes to a smaller house, at 6 Foyle Road in Greenwich. Some time after Herman had married and moved to Reading, and Mabel had married Ernest Biss, Mary moved to Poole in Dorset where she died in December 1917.

Plate 1. St George-in-the-East Church, Stepney, where George Burney, his brother and five sisters were baptised.

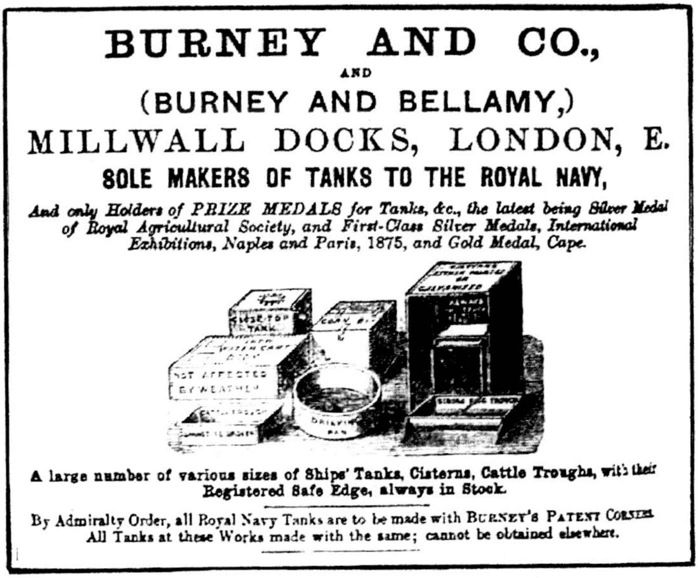

Plate 2. Advertisement for Burney & Co products.

i

Plate 3. All Saints Church, Poplar where George Burney, was a member of the Vestry in the 1850s and 1860s.

Plate 4. The Crown Inn, Loughton, c1890, where Burney and his 'gang' had lunch in January 1878, after pulling fences down.
(Lopping Hall is shown in the background).

Plate 5. Terracotta panel of 'Loughton Lopper', above the entrance to Lopping Hall. George Burney was one of the first Trustees of the Lopping Endowment.

Plate 6. Powell's Forest, Buckhurst Hill, where George Burney and his 'gang' pulled down fences in January 1878.

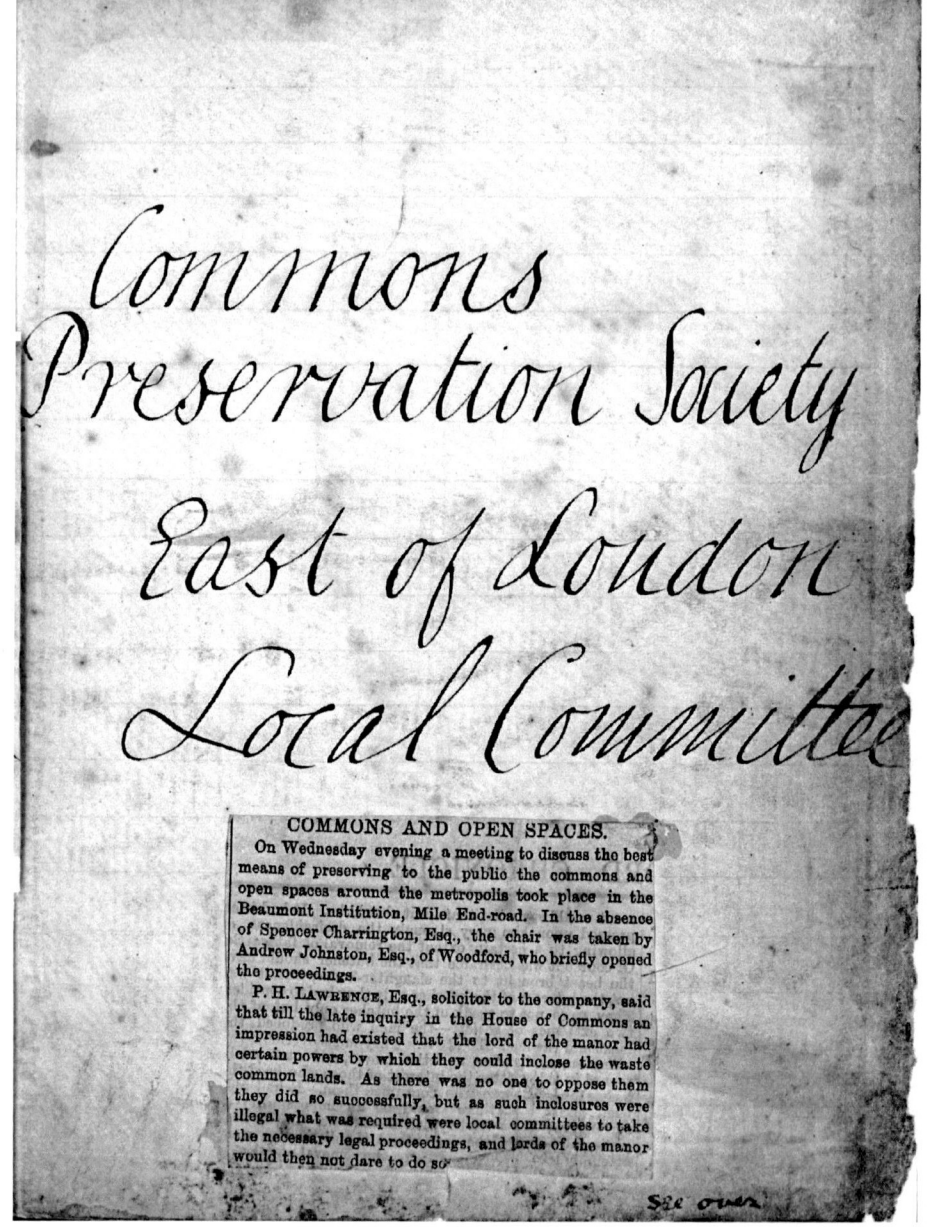

Plate 7. Title page of the Minute Book 1866–69, of the Commons Preservation Society, East of London Committee.

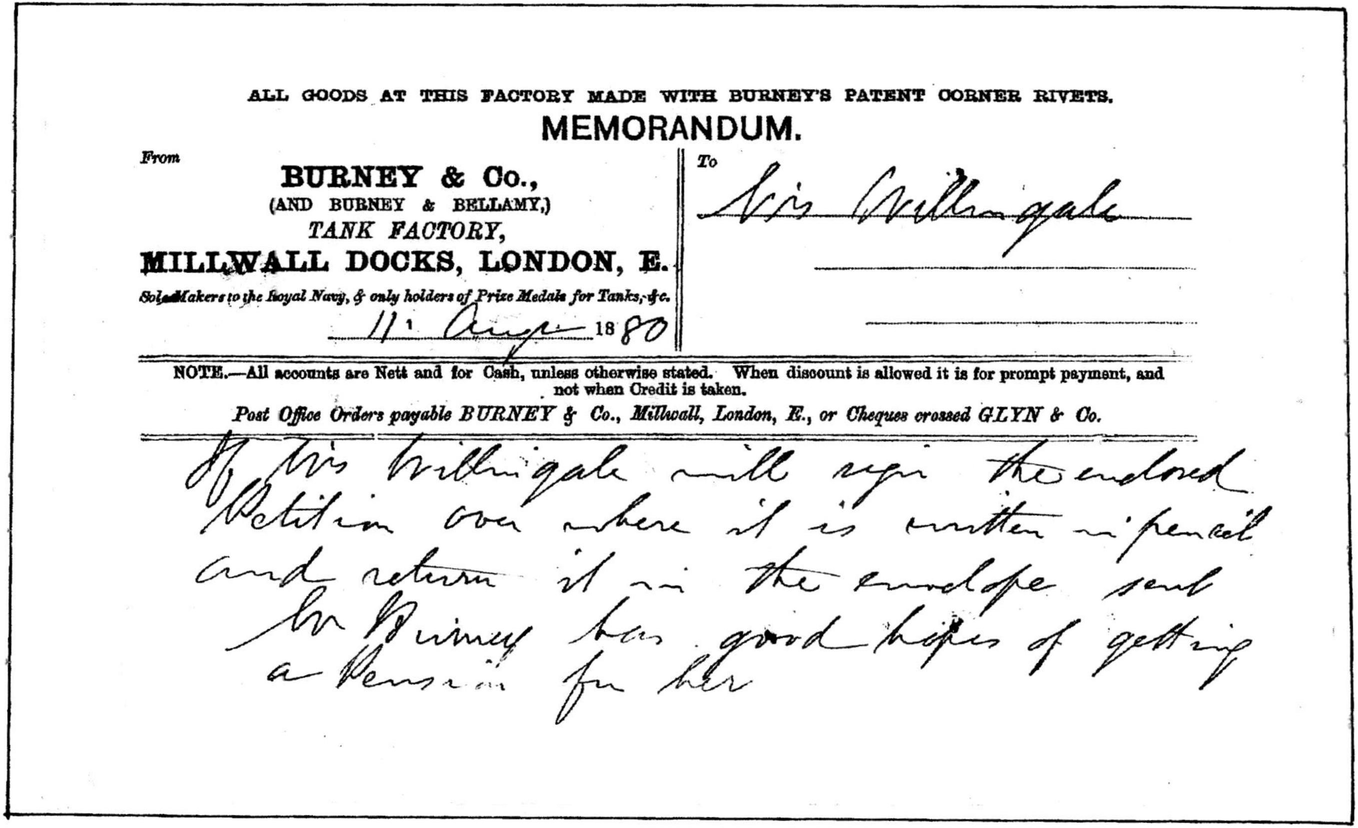

ALL GOODS AT THIS FACTORY MADE WITH BURNEY'S PATENT CORNER RIVETS.

MEMORANDUM.

From

BURNEY & Co.,
(AND BURNEY & BELLAMY,)
TANK FACTORY,
MILLWALL DOCKS, LONDON, E.
Sole Makers to the Royal Navy, & only holders of Prize Medals for Tanks, &c.

11 Aug 1880

To Mrs Willingale

NOTE.—All accounts are Nett and for Cash, unless otherwise stated. When discount is allowed it is for prompt payment, and not when Credit is taken.

Post Office Orders payable BURNEY & Co., Millwall, London, E., or Cheques crossed GLYN & Co.

If Mrs Willingale will sign the enclosed
Petition over where it is written in pencil
and return it in the envelope sent
Mr Burney has good hopes of getting
a Pension for her

Plate 8 . Memorandum from George Burney to Mrs Willingale, August 1880, indicating that he hopes to obtain a pension for her.

EPPING FOREST.

THE PRESENTATION OF TESTIMONIALS AND ADDRESSES

To Sir THOS. J. NELSON, Lieut.-Col. PALMER, J. T. BEDFORD, Esq., W. G. S. SMITH, Esq., AND E. J. DANIELL, Esq., will take place at a

PUBLIC LUNCHEON IN THE LARGE PAVILION OF THE FOREST HOTEL, CHINGFORD, ON SATURDAY, JUNE 12, AT 4 P.M.

Sir ANTONIO BRADY, J.P., F.G.S., Verderer, in the Chair. Tickets, 6s., or Double Tickets (Lady and Gentleman), 10s. 6d., may be had before the 8th June, on application to Captain John East Gray, Clova Road, Forest Gate, E., or Mr. Charles John Glass, Bocking House, Walthamstow, Hon. Secretaries to the Epping Forest Testimonial Fund.

THE FOREST HOTEL.

TABLE D'HOTE LUNCHEONS (at separate tables) Soups followed by Cold Collation served in Tea Room, 2/6.
TABLE D'HOTE DINNER (at separate tables) Soups, Fish, Entrees, Joints, Sweets, Cheese, Dessert, from 4 to 8 o'clock, 4/-; in Private Rooms, 5/-

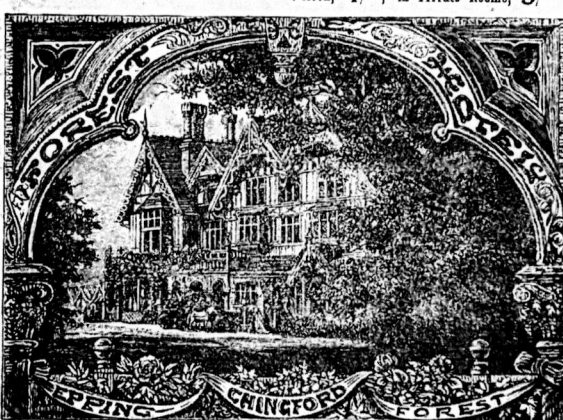

The Great DINING HALL, Lofty, Spacious, and Sumptuously Furnished; For CEREMONIAL BANQUETS, MASONIC, CLUB, and other Festivals, ANNIVERSARY CELEBRATIONS, and PUBLIC DINNERS.

The PAVILION, In the Grounds of the Hotel, for LARGE ASSEMBLIES, "BEAN FEASTS," TRADE DINNERS, SUNDAY SCHOOL and CHARITABLE TREATS, &c.

Will accommodate 600 adults or 800 children.

In the Hotel Department, well ventilated and comfortable Bedrooms, and a series of the pleasantest private Sitting-rooms in England.

The FOREST HOTEL is situated amidst the most delightful scenery of Epping Forest, and is close to the Chingford Station, about half-an-hour's pleasant journey from Liverpool Street, City, or an easy distance by road from any part of London.

HORSES AND CARRIAGES.

THE EPPING FOREST (BURNEY) TESTIMONIAL FUND.

A numerous and influential COMMITTEE OF GENTLEMEN has been formed for the purpose of publicly recognising the energetic and continuous services during the last twenty-five years of Mr. GEORGE BURNEY, of Millwall, in preserving the rights of the people to the free use of the Forest.

EXECUTIVE COMMITTEE.—J. H. ANDERSON, Esq., Queen Victoria Street (*Chairman*).
W. Askew, Esq., 1, Queen's Gate, Victoria Park, E.   Bradshaw Brown, Esq., 16, London Street, E.C.
J. H. Clews, Esq., Tredegar Road, Bow.   T. G. Fletcher, Esq., St. Ann's Wharf, Limehouse, E.

All interested in, or benefited by, the successful result of these labours are requested to apply for a copy of the Committee's Circular, or any other information, to the undersigned, at 5, Great Winchester Street, E. C.

W. J. WALTHEW, *Secretary*.

Plate 9. Advertisement for the testimonial Lunch at the Forest Hotel, 1880.

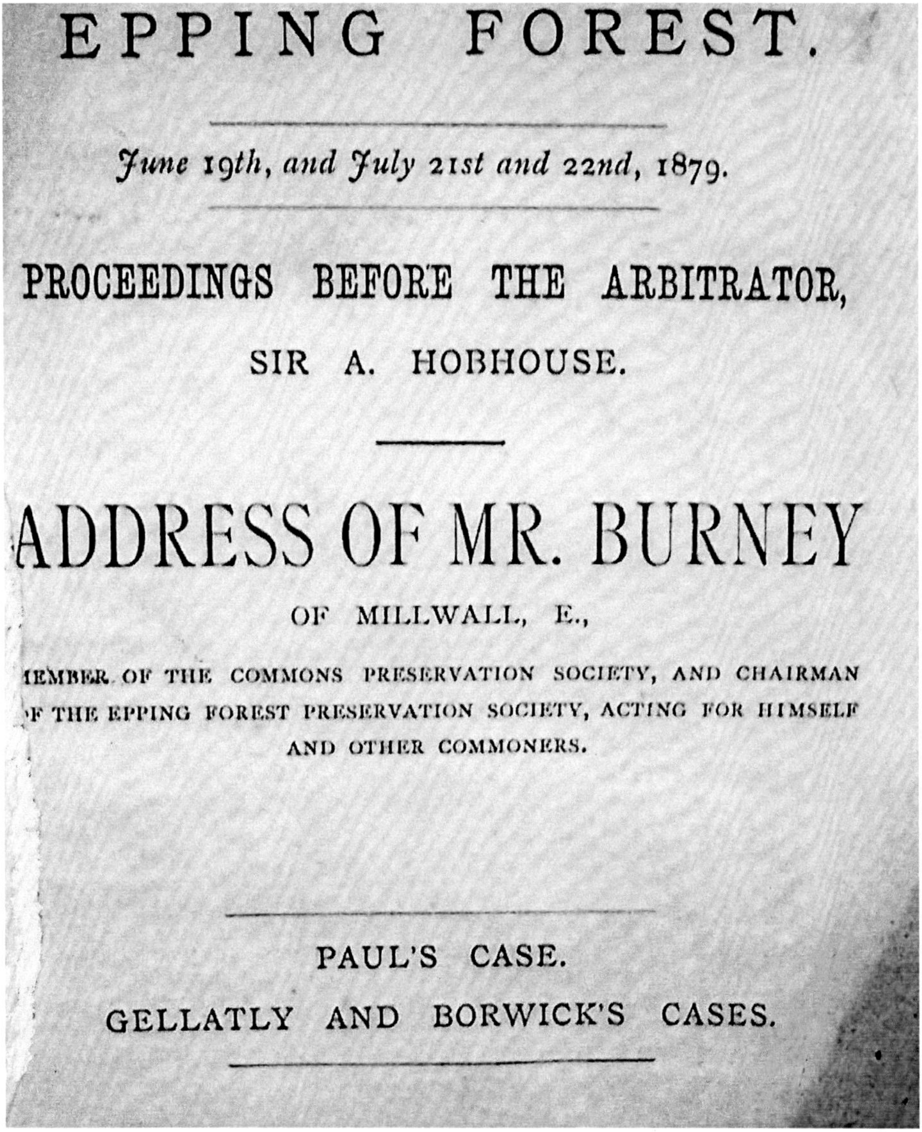

EPPING FOREST.

June 19th, and July 21st and 22nd, 1879.

PROCEEDINGS BEFORE THE ARBITRATOR,

SIR A. HOBHOUSE.

ADDRESS OF MR. BURNEY

OF MILLWALL, E.,

MEMBER OF THE COMMONS PRESERVATION SOCIETY, AND CHAIRMAN OF THE EPPING FOREST PRESERVATION SOCIETY, ACTING FOR HIMSELF AND OTHER COMMONERS.

PAUL'S CASE.

GELLATLY AND BORWICK'S CASES.

Plate 10. Burney Pamphlet for his evidence to the Arbitrator in 1879.

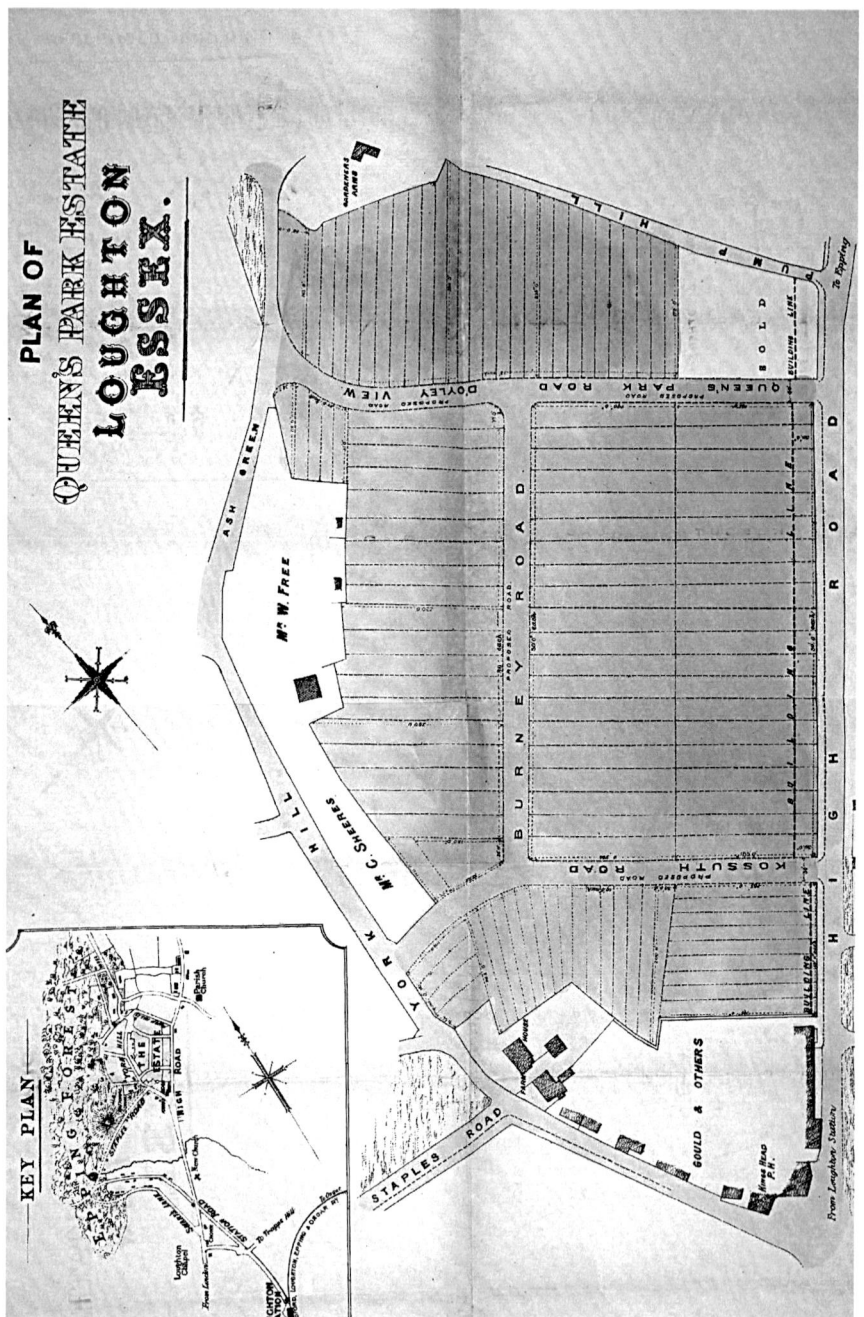

Plate 11. Plan for the Queen's Park Estate, Loughton, sold in March 1886. (Reproduced by courtesy of the Essex Record Office, ref SALE/B490.)

Appendices

APPENDIX 1: PARODY UPON SCOTT'S 'LOCHINVAR'

A parody upon Sir Walter Scott's 'Lochinvar', by John Bedford, addressed to George Burney:

THE MODERN LOCHINVAR

O, Gallant George Burney's come out of the west,
To claim his true rights in the People's Forest;
And, save saw and hammer, he weapon had none,
He rode all unarm'd; but he rode not alone,
For eighty good fellows, some young and some old,
Have come at the call of George Burney the Bold.

They stay'd not for drink and they stay'd not for fun,
They cross'd the bright greensward where road there was none;
And, when they alighted at Borwick's red gate,
They at once set to work before it got late,
For lords and grantees, as George Burney saw,
Had kept up their fences despite the law.

So boldly they entered with hammer and saw,
And down went the fences condemned by the law.
Then spake two Policemen who came from Old Ford,
(For the poor craven grantees said never a word)
'O come ye to buy this enclosure for gold,
Or to pull down the fences, George Burney the Bold?'

'The great Corporation a long suit have tried,
Law rolls like a river but ebbs like its tide,
And now I have come with these good friends of mine –
Who shall have a good dinner and plenty of wine –
To show the grantees they had better by far
Submit to the verdict according to law.'

So at it they went, these good men and true,
And, as their own long coats, the Bobbies looked blue;
And so sharp were their saws, and their arms were so strong,
That to fell all the fences did not take them long.
So three miles of fences were felled in one day,
And with three ringing cheers they went home on their way.

There was cursing and swearing when up rose the sun,
And this bold deed was seen that George Burney had done;
And Borwick's loud tongue waxed louder and louder,
And his wrath rose as fast as the famed Baking Powder.
So daring in deed and so fearless of gold,
Have you e'er heard of man like George Burney the Bold?

APPENDIX 2: SOURCES

Barclay-Johnston Collection on Epping Forest (London Metropolitan Archives, cat. CLA/077/E/04/02).

Bedford, John, *The Story of the Preservation of Epping Forest* (London, 1882).

Burney Pamphlets:

 Epping Forest to be saved at Last, c 1870 (PAM 10831, Guildhall Library, City of London).

 Epping Forest to be Saved without a Corn Tax, February 1872 (British Library, Gen Ref Coll, Shelfmark 10350.aa.51).

 The Present State of the Epping Forest Question, December 1876 (Epping Forest Special Collection No 3, Essex Field Club).

 The Present State of the Epping Forest Question, May 1877 (PAM 3240, Guildhall Library, City of London).

 Public Notice, re Commoners' Rights in Epping Forest, 1878.(PAM 11953, Guildhall Library, City of London).

 Epping Forest, Proceedings before the Arbitrator, Address of Mr Burney, 1879 (PAM 4573, Guildhall Library, City of London).

 The Lopping Rights in Loughton, c1880 (PAM 605, Guildhall Library, City of London).

Census Records:1851, 1861, 1871, 1881, 1891, 1901, 1911.

Commons Preservation Society, Minute Book of East of London Local Committee, 1866-1869 (LB of Tower Hamlets Archives, cat. TH/8557).

Corporation of London, Coal, Corn & Finance Committee Minute Books 1884 & 1885 (London Metropolitan Archives, cat. COL/CC/CCF/02/050 & 051).

Court of Chancery: *Chilton* v. *Burney*. Writ issued 25 January 1878: Statement of claim delivered 11 May 1878, statement of defence delivered 20 June 1878 (London Metropolitan Archives, cat. CLA/077/01/016/011).

Deed: 1876 Covenant to keep up river wall on Millwall Embankment (including part through Burney's wharf) (LB of Tower Hamlets Archives).
Epping Forest Arbitration, Section 13, Lopping Rights in the Manor and Parish of Loughton (1880–1881).
Essex Field Club, *Journal*, vol. 4, 1885, obituary.
London Borough of Greenwich, Cemeteries Department. Burial register for Greenwich cemetery. Burney grave No 4659B.

Newspapers:
 East London Observer: 2 May 1885, obituary.
 Evening News: 25 June 1946, Burney's axe.
 The Standard:
  14 January 1868, 'New St Luke's Church'.
  1 August 1885, Sale of property.
  20 March 1886, Sale of property in Loughton.
 The Stratford Express:
  19 January 1878, 'Destroying Fences on Forest Land'.
  5 July 1946, Burney's Axe.
 The Times:
  23 April 1867 p.6, 'Epping Forest meeting'.
  25 January 1878, Law Report.
  25 May 1878, Law Report.
  16 June 1878, Sale of freehold of 'The Limes', Greenwich.
  14 June 1880, p.12, 'Epping Forest'.
  4 May 1882, Epping Forest, Leading article.
  25 April 1884, p.10, 'Court of Common Council'.
  28 April 1885, Notice of death of George Burney.
  12 May 1914, Marriage of Mabel Biss, née Burney, to Charles Steel.
 The Woodford Times: 19 January 1878. 'Destruction of Fences by Londoners'.

Metropolitan Board of Works, Report of Proceedings of the Board with regard to Epping Forest, 1871 (British Library, cat. YC.2012.a.7555(35)).
Rate Book, All Saints, Poplar, 1851 (LB of Tower Hamlets Archives).
Rate Books for Loughton 1881-83 (Essex Record Office, cat. D/ULo/2/1/4/1, D/ULo/2/1/2/1, and D/ULo/2/1/4/2).
St George-in-the-East, Stepney, parish registers (LB of Tower Hamlets, Archives).
Select Committee on Royal Forests (Essex), Minutes of Evidence, George Burney examined, 7 May 1863.
Survey of London vols. 43 & 44: Poplar & Blackwall. (1994).
Venn, J, *Alumni Cantabrigienses*, 1940 edition.
Waller, W C, *Loughton in Essex, the history of the manor and parish, and transcripts of wills*, (1889–1900).

APPENDIX 3: CENSUS RECORDS

1851 Census
George Burney
Age: 32
Date of birth: 1818
Born: Middlesex
Address: Town Arch Cottage, Old Ford Road, Bow, Middlesex
Occupation: Tank manufacturer employing 22 hands
Harriet (maiden name not stated), wife, 50 years
Emma Turtle house servant 23

1861 Census
George Burney
Age: 42
Date of birth: 1818
Born: Middlesex
Address: 79 Stainsby Road, All Saints, Poplar, Tower Hamlets
Occupation: Iron Tank manufacturer
Mary Ann Jane Vaughan, wife, 25 years (b. 1836)
James Spencer, father-in-law (widower), 49 (Timber merchant)
Eliza Cates, servant, 25
Emma Tullstone, servant, 46

1871 Census
George Burney
Age: 52
Date of birth: 1818
Born: Middlesex
Address: 26 Crooms Hill, Greenwich, Kent
Occupation: Tank manufacturer employing 70 men and 20 boys.
Mary Ann Jane Vaughan, wife, 34 years
Eleanor, daughter, 6
Herman Kossuth, son, 9
James Spencer, father-in-law (widower), 59 (commercial traveller)
Mary Lark, servant (nurse)
Eliza Buck, servant (cook)
Mary Buck, servant (housemaid)

1881 Census
George Burney
Age: 62
Date of birth: 1818
Born: Middlesex
Address: The Limes, Greenwich, Kent
Occupation: Iron Tank manufacturer employing 120 hands.
Mary Ann Jane Vaughan, wife, 43 years
Herman Kossuth, son (law student), 19
Eleanor, daughter (scholar), 16
Mabel, daughter (scholar), 7
James Spencer, father-in-law (widower), 69
Emily Binns, companion, 32
Mary Armstrong, visitor, 19
Ellen Patten, servant (cook), 24
Emily Cook, servant (housemaid), 18
Fanny Hensman, servant (housemaid), 19

1891 Census
Herman Kossuth Burney (son)
Age: 29
Date of birth: 1862
Address: C K Brewery, Charlton Kings, Cheltenham, Gloucestershire.
Occupation: Brewer
Wilfred Wire, 23, Brewer
Susannah Spencer, 63, Widow, Housekeeper

Living at 6 Foyle Road, Greenwich, Kent.
Mary Ann Jane Vaughan Burney (widow), 53
Mabel Burney (daughter), 17
James Spencer (Mary's father), 79
Elizabeth Bass (servant), 20
Eleanor Mary Burney (daughter), 26. was visitor to Alfred English in Stoke-on-Trent, Staffordshire on day of census.

1901 Census
6 Foyle Road, Greenwich, Kent
Herman Kossuth Burney (Head – Son), 39, Barrister/Solicitor
Mary Ann Jane Vaughan Burney (widow – mother), 64

Eleanor Burney (sister/daughter), 36
Mabel Burney (sister/ daughter), 27
Kate Laming (servant), 20

1911 Census
Glensdale, Seldown Road, Poole, Dorset
Mary Ann Jane Vaughan Burney (widow), 73
Eleanor Mary Burney (daug.), 46
Mabel Constance Biss (née Burney) (daughter), 37, widow
Annie Allner (servant)

Note. Mary Ann Burney, George Burney's wife, died at 3 Belvedere Crescent, Parkstone, Poole, Dorset, on 31 December 1917.

Westcombe Road, Reading, Berks
Herman Burney (son of George), 49, married, Hospital Secretary
Violet Messent Burney (née Canton), 37, wife, born Southsea, Hants.
Alfred Collyer (servant)

Note. Herman Burney married Violet (daughter of George Canton) at Emmanuel Church, Hampstead, on 7 April 1906. They do not appear to have had any children. He was Secretary to the Royal Berkshire Hospital. Herman moved in retirement to Kingland Road, Poole, Dorset, where he died on 1 May 1938. He left £7,358.